PRAISE F

"Paul Ferrini is an important teacher in the new millennium. Reading his work has been a major awakening for me."— Iyanla Vanzant

"These words embody tolerance, universality, love and compassion— hallmarks of all Great Teachings. They turn our attention inward to our own divine nature, instead of diverting it outward. Paul Ferrini is a modern-day Kahlil Gibran—poet, mystic, visionary, teller of truth." Larry Dossey, M.D., author of *Healing Words: The Power of Prayer and the Practice of Medicine.*

"Paul Ferrini leads us skillfully and courageously beyond shame, blame and attachment to our wounds into the depths of self-forgiveness. His work is a must-read for all people who are ready to take responsibility for their own healing." John Bradshaw, author of *Family Secrets.*

"A breath of fresh air in an often musty and cluttered domain. With sweetness, clarity, and simplicity we are directed to the truth within. I read this book whenever my heart directs, which is often." Pat Rodegast, author of *Emmanuel's Book I, II and III.*

"Paul Ferrini's writing is authentic, delightful and wise. It reconnects the reader to the Spirit Within, to that place where even our deepest wounds can be healed." Joan Borysenko, Ph.D., author of *Guilt is the Teacher, Love is the Answer.*

"I feel that this work comes from a continuous friendship with the deepest part of the Self. I trust its wisdom." Coleman Barks, poet and translator.

"Paul Ferrini's wonderful books show a way to walk lightly with joy on planet earth." Gerald Jampolsky, M.D., author of *Love is Letting Go of Fear.*

Book Design by Paul Ferrini
and Lisa Carta

Library of Congress Control Number
2006935628

ISBN # 1-879159-67-8

Heartways Press, Inc.
9 Phillips Street, Greenfield MA 01301
www.heartwayspress.com

Manufactured in the United States of America

LOVE
IS MY GOSPEL

*The Radical Teachings of Jesus
on Healing, Empowerment
and the Call to Serve*

PAUL FERRINI

TABLE OF CONTENTS

Preface

Much is misunderstood about the teachings of Jesus. The Jesus whom we know through the Gospels is but a glimpse of the real man, his teachings and his passion.

So be it. Much is inevitably lost when those who write and retell his message do not have the same level of understanding as their teacher. Even more is lost in translation.

Some try to find insight into the man and his teachings through alternative Biblical sources. Yet the Gnostic Gospels and other scriptural fragments shed little additional light on the man or his teaching.

Regardless of how many Bibles or scriptures you have read, there comes a time when you must go beyond the words into a direct experience of the teacher and his teaching.

Consider these words then but an invitation to go deeper and invite the teacher into your heart. And remember that the one who will speak to you is not the Jesus of Biblical times, but the Jesus of today.

As innovative as Jesus' message was, it was still shaped by the religion and the culture of the era in which he lived. Jesus was a Jew speaking to Jews at a time when Roman values, culture and military strength dominated the world.

Now Jesus abides in the realms of Spirit. He is neither a Jew nor a Christian, but a living presence whose empowerment teaching goes beyond the limits of time, place or history.

His message today is clear, direct, and completely resonant with the core teachings we find in the gospels. It lacks only the fear-based language and the millennium fever of that time.

I feel blessed to be a student of these teachings and to share them with you. Nevertheless, I encourage you not to accept anything I say, nor indeed, anything he says, without testing it to see if it is true and helpful to you.

For truth is always helpful, although it often helps people in different ways, but that which is untrue cannot help anyone, regardless of the promises it makes.

So open your mind and listen with your heart. Put these teachings to work in your life and you will know if they serve you or not.

If they don't, toss them away. You are responsible for the teachings you accept and you cannot accept a teaching that does not bring you greater insight and empower you to live a more loving life.

If, on the other hand, these teachings serve you, pass them along to others who can use them to open their hearts, awaken their minds, and step into the fullness of their creative power.

For the world we live in needs many compassionate leaders and witnesses to the truth. And now is the time for each one of us to stand up and do what we came here to do.

May the light of Christ shine in your heart and in your eyes now and for all time.

Love and Blessings,

Paul Jerrini

1

Christ Consciousness and the Barriers to Love

"I am the way and the truth and the life."
(JOHN 14:6)

These words could be spoken by Jesus because he had awakened to the Truth about himself. He had discovered and claimed his divine origin.

Jesus does not make the statement because he wishes to be special. This is the statement of a man who has come into the fullness of his being.

He has achieved his spiritual potential. He has joined with God and can act as a messenger of the divine.

He holds out the same possibility for me and for you.

Yet Jesus also says, *"No one comes to the Father except through me."*

There are two ways this can be interpreted. The way it is usually interpreted is that we have to believe in the sole divinity of Jesus to have a relationship with God.

The other way to interpret it is to say we have to become the Son of God, or enter into Christ Consciousness, to know God. That is what Jesus did. He became the Christ, the anointed one, through direct communion with God. Jesus became a spiritual master and we are asked to do the same.

*"One who believes in me will do the works that I do
and, in fact, will do greater works than these."*
(JOHN 14:12)

The teaching of Jesus is an empowerment teaching. Its purpose is to help us awaken to the truth and become fully empowered. We listen deeply to the words of Jesus in order to internalize his teachings and live in the consciousness from which those teachings come.

Jesus tells us clearly that we can awaken too. The potential to live in Christ Consciousness is there in each one of us.

Now, as you read his words, ask yourself "Do I believe this?

Do I believe that I can overcome the world, as Jesus did? Do I believe I can overcome shame, selfishness, pride, greed, envy? Do I believe that I can walk through my fears and stand in my power unafraid of what anyone will say about me or do to me? Do I believe that I can connect radically to my Creator's love and learn to be myself fully, completely, confidently and fearlessly?"

If you answer, "Yes," I congratulate you. You have taken the first step on your path to full empowerment.

You cannot start on your journey unless you know where you are going and believe that it is possible to get there.

THE SPIRITUAL MASTERY PROCESS

The Spiritual Mastery Process is a three-fold process. The three steps in this Process are as follows:

- Healing
- Empowerment
- Service

Healing is the first step in the process. We are all wounded and must discover and heal from our core wounds. These wounds block our connection to our core self and our divine Source.

As we heal, we reestablish our connection to our core self. This enables us to know and experience ourselves as an authentic person who has unique gifts to offer the world. *Empowerment* is therefore the second step in the process. During this phase we stop the patterns of self betrayal in our life, begin to trust our guidance and learn to develop and express our gifts.

The third step in the Mastery process is *Service*. Once we have experienced healing and empowerment, we become capable of helping others with similar core wounds to heal those wounds and to discover and value their gifts. In this third step, we give to others the kind of help that we received from mentors and helpers when we were healing. The process of giving back is essential to the collective healing process, as it is the way that the world is redeemed, one heart at a time.

In that sense, the healing of human consciousness is inextricably linked to our own healing process. As we wake up, so do our brothers and sisters.

Jesus was well aware of this process. That is why he worked so intensely with his disciples. He knew that it would be through them that the work of healing and empowerment would be passed on.

You cannot remain small, insignificant, invisible and be a student of these teachings.

The teachings ask you to expand your idea of who you are. You are not just a bag of skin and bones with emotional needs and an ego structure.

You are a unique expression of the Creator's love and wisdom. You are a Servant of God waiting to be born.

Jesus did not come here to tell us he was the only Christ. He came to show us the way to Christhood so that each one of us could do our part in serving the greater good.

Just as "smallness" is an illusion, so is "grandiosity."

Just as you can't get away with believing that you are unimportant and insignificant, you also cannot get away with believing that you are greater than anyone else.

What makes you important and significant makes everyone else equally so.

In other words, no one has more Christ potential than anyone else. Those who remove the barriers to Love become the pure expressions of Love. It is that simple.

What are the barriers?

Pride is a barrier. Hatred is a barrier. Judgment is a barrier. Envy is a barrier. Selfishness is a barrier. Greed is a barrier. Shame or unworthiness is a barrier.

There are many barriers. You know them as well as I do. And you encounter these barriers not just in the minds and hearts of others, but in your own consciousness as well.

UNWORTHINESS IS
THE GREATEST BARRIER

Most people struggle with a deep sense of unworthiness.
Moreover, they put Jesus up on a pedestal. They say, "He is
special. I cannot possibly be like him."

They make their teacher into a savior or a God. They believe
"he will do for me what I cannot do for myself."

If you are one of these people, ask yourself "Do I really want
a co-dependent relationship with Jesus? Do I want him to do
everything for me or do I want to learn from him so that I can
make good choices on my own? Do I want to be independent
and empowered or do I want to give my power away to someone else?"

These are important questions.

To be a disciple does not require giving away your free will.
To be sure, it requires being humble and willing to learn, but it
does not mean slavery or submission to a person or to an idea.
Accepting anyone as a savior reinforces your unworthiness. It
keeps you in a dependent position.

Any teacher that would control or limit your freedom or take
away your power to decide for yourself is no spiritual teacher, but
an imposter. Many cult leaders fit that bill.

Jesus wants to empower you, not to take your power away.
Let us be clear on that.

A teacher of empowerment knows that he has succeeded
when the student is strong enough and skillful enough to stand
on his own. Moreover, if he learns to stand in the fullness of his
power, he is capable of empowering others and this is how the
teaching spreads exponentially.

One teacher can empower many.

So don't be confused on this point. Don't think it is okay for you to give away your power because you are giving it to Jesus.

It's not okay. Jesus doesn't need your power. It is not what he wants. He wants you to stand in your power so that you can shine your light and give your gifts to the world.

Standing in your power is not to be powerful over others. It is the power of the Self to be Itself. If you give your power to others, you cannot be your authentic Self. And then you will be afraid to stand in your truth and be a Servant of Love.

A SERVANT OF LOVE

To be a Servant of Love, you must be yourself fully. You must be a unique vessel for Spirit.

God is not looking for carbon copies. Jesus is not asking you to be Jesus.

Have the courage to be you. Speak your truth. Do not let the laws and customs of the world prevent you from becoming the one you are here to be.

In other words: "Show up! Stop hiding your light under a bushel. Stop hugging the wall and join the dance."

You didn't come here to be an ornament. You came here to love, to teach and to inspire, as he did.

That is what Jesus is asking of you.

He wants you to be as great in your own right as he was in his. Not only that! He knows that you can be.

All you have to do is take back your power. Stop being a victim. Stop making excuses.

You are not weak. You are not a fly on the wall. You are not invisible.

Leave this lie behind. Your teacher is calling you to a greater truth. Do you hear the call? Will you answer it?

It's your choice.

GUILT IS ANOTHER BARRIER

Perhaps you feel unworthy because you have made mistakes in the past. Yet those mistakes cannot cut you off from your Creator's love, unless you refuse to acknowledge them and correct them.

Every day, Jesus asked you to pray "Father, forgive me my trespasses as I forgive those who trespass against me." (Matthew 6:12)

He knows that you are going to make mistakes. He knows that you are going to trespass against others and/or allow them to trespass against you.

But he asks you not to let the mistake go uncorrected. Every trespass must be rectified.

If you are attacking, look at your anger and frustration. Pull your claws in. Give others space and stop trying to control them.

If you are being attacked, look at your fear and learn to say "No" to those who would control you. Stand up for yourself.

If you are imposing on others, learn to step back. If you are retreating, learn to step forward.

He didn't ask you to make these corrections once per month or once per week. He asked to you do this constantly.

The forgiveness prayer must be done throughout the day to correct our errors and restore balance in our hearts and our relationships.

Why do we say the prayer?

Because we are carrying shame and we need to reclaim our innocence.

Because we are holding grievances and we need to restore our awareness of the innocence of others.

Some people think that it is enough to believe in the divinity of Jesus. They don't think they need to do the everyday work of forgiveness that Jesus gave to them.

Well, they are mistaken. Jesus told us "If you keep my commandments, you will abide in my love." (John 15:10)

That means practice.

The practice of forgiveness leads to the experience of equality. Without equality, there can be no justice in this world. True justice is possible only when we see and treat each other as equals.

Justice is a condition of the Kingdom. It rarely exists in this world.

Yet each of us brings the Kingdom as we offer forgiveness to ourselves and to each other.

These are the teachings of the Master. Let us be humble and learn them.

They will transform our lives.

WOUNDS

Jesus was wounded. He was crucified by the world. He did not run away from his earthly challenge and we must not run away from ours.

We come into this experience with certain lessons to learn. We feel unworthy. We feel unequal.

Our parents, our siblings, our teachers, our friends do not always treat us kindly or accept us as we are.

Some of us are orphans. We lost a parent early in life. Some of our family members have been injured or murdered at the hands of others.

Some have taken the life of another; some have taken their own lives. Some were abused, physically or emotionally, by parents or caretakers, siblings, spouses, or even by total strangers.

The human world is often not a friendly or a kind place. People who have been hurt tend to hurt others. They do to others what has been done to them.

You cannot be in the world and not be wounded.

The size of the wound may or may not determine the amount of hurt that it brings or the degree of desire for healing.

Even small wounds can cause great hurt. Even large wounds can heal quickly.

It all depends on us.

If you deny the wound, it cannot heal.

Jesus did not deny his wounds. He said: "Father, forgive them for they know not what they do." (Luke 23:34)

He did not deny the wound. But he did not hold onto it either.

22

The wound is an invitation to heal an old unworthiness. It may be an unworthiness you were born with, or it may be an unworthiness you developed in childhood.

It does not matter when or where the wound occurred.

To heal you must acknowledge the wound and you must not hold onto it. That means that ultimately you must forgive yourself and the one who attacked you.

If you pretend the wound does not exist, you will not heal it. You will be walking around wounded, and everything you say or do will be driven by the anger and unworthiness attached to the unhealed wound.

When we are wounded we do one of two things. Either we attack others (externalize the wound), or we attack ourselves (internalize the wound).

In the former case, the victim becomes a victimizer and re-enacts the cycle of violence. In the latter case, the victim remains a victim and attracts another victimizer, thus deepening the pain of the wound.

Unhealed wounds fuel the cycle of violence and create more and more pain in the world. Wars are the creation of wounded adults in denial of their emotional wounds.

Jesus asked us to feel the pain and heal the wound.

He asked us to feel our own pain. He asked us to feel the pain of others, including the pain of those we attack and the pain of those who attack us.

You can't stay wounded if you feel your own pain. You can't stay wounded if you feel the pain of the one you attack or the one who attacks you.

Indeed, feeling the pain of the wound is the road to healing.

Once you feel the pain of the wound, you have acknowledged it, and then you can begin the process of forgiving yourself and the one who attacked you.

When people who have hurt us take responsibility for their actions and express remorse for the pain they have caused, forgiving them is natural.

We all know how to forgive if we have been forgiven. But if we have never been forgiven, we may not be able to forgive ourselves or others, and then the wound will not be healed.

Forgiveness is a process we are engaged in every day and every hour of the day. It is one of the core spiritual practices associated with the teachings of Jesus.

When we give ourselves the gift of forgiveness, we take ourselves off the cross and we create a loving space where our wounds can heal. When we give others the gift of forgiveness, we take them down from the cross, dress their wounds and set them free on their journey of healing and empowerment.

Those whom we forgive learn from us how to forgive others and themselves. Thus, the gift is strengthened and affirmed, bringing peace to our hearts and our world.

SHAME IS A BARRIER

The work of self-forgiveness is deeper than we think.

Some people are so ashamed they are convinced that anyone who might learn their deep, dark secret would hate them and condemn them. They believe the Master himself would reject them and that surely God has given up on them.

Yet Jesus tells us otherwise: "Forgive and you will be forgiven." (Luke 6:38)

If you are one of these who is holding on to a terrible secret, your teacher invites you to release your burden. Confess your secret and ask for forgiveness. For mistakes are not to be hidden, but brought out of the darkness into the light of day for correction.

Ask yourself this question now: "What forgiveness could I give or receive to clean the slate of past errors, so that I could once again open my heart to receive my Creator's love?"

And now offer that forgiveness to yourself and to anyone from you have been withholding forgiveness as you say the prayer "Father, forgive me my trespasses as I forgive those who trespass against me."

Let your heart open as you pray. Pray that you find the willingness to let go of your shame and your grievances.

*Christ has opened the door already.
If you do not feel his love,
it is because you have closed the door.
It is you, then, who must open it.*

There are many reasons why we close our hearts. We have been hurt. We have hurt others. We are angry at others. We are angry at ourselves.

Perhaps we are also angry at Jesus or at God. That is not uncommon.

Jesus does not reject you because you have rejected him.

He does not love you *with conditions.* He loves you *without conditions.*

That means that his arms are always outstretched toward you. There is never a time when you cannot reach out and take his hand.

His refuge knows no limits. It is deeper than any depth and wider than any width. There is nothing you could have done or said or believed that could cut you off from his love.

If you doubt this, test him. If you have even the tiniest willingness to come into the lap of his love, he will match it tenfold.

Jesus tells us over and over again that the Son is like the Father. He is merely reflecting the magnificence of God's eternal, steadfast Love for us.

No, Jesus will not reject you. And God cannot reject you. The door to the sanctuary is always open.

2

Two Teachings

There are two teachings. One empowers.
The other enslaves.

Which, do you suppose, is the one he offers?

If Jesus were in the world today, he would speak to us differently from the way he speaks to us in the gospels.

He would speak to us as brothers and sisters, as equals. He would not seek to manipulate or control us through fear or browbeat us with the image of a vengeful God who threatens to punish us for our mistakes.

He would address us in the language of love. Jesus seeks to guide us, not to punish us. He seeks to bring us closer to God, not to push us away from Him.

The teachings of fear have no place
in the gospel of love.

If Jesus of Nazareth was ever unclear on this point, be sure that Jesus the Christ, the anointed one, knows and proclaims this truth now and for all time.

For we cannot have it both ways. Either this is a teaching of love or it is a teaching of fear.

Either God is loving and compassionate or He is not.

Put simply, we all have to make a choice about which God we want to worship. That choice will determine, for a large part, whether we follow the teaching of vicarious atonement or the teaching of empowerment.

TWO VIEWS OF THE WORLD

If you believe in an angry God who will punish you for wrongdoing and you have done wrong, like most people, then you need a savior. You need someone to intervene with God on your behalf. This is the *teaching of vicarious atonement.*

If you believe in a loving and compassionate God and you make mistakes, like the rest of us, you don't need a savior. You can communicate with God directly and ask for forgiveness. This is the *teaching of empowerment.*

This teaching of vicarious atonement states that Jesus is the only Son of God. He died for our sins. If we believe in him, we will be saved. If we don't, we will perish.

Like God, Jesus is all-powerful. He could have stopped the crucifixion but chose not to, because it was God's will. By the same token, he could have stopped the Holocaust and other examples of human cruelty, but chose not to.

This teaching of empowerment states that Jesus is a Child of God and so is each one of us. Jesus was an advanced spiritual master who came here to help us learn to love God and each other. He was the greatest of all the Hebrew prophets and teachers. Jesus was a role model for us and, if we are willing to follow in his footsteps, we too can awaken spiritually and become teachers of love who inspire others and help to create a better, more just world.

The teaching of vicarious atonement says that the world can be saved only by God or Jesus.

The teaching of empowerment says that the world is redeemed—not from on high—but through the actions of wise, caring human beings who are responsible for their actions and seek the common good.

The teaching of vicarious atonement says that God loves and rewards those who obey his will and that of his Son. All others are punished and denied entrance to the kingdom.

The teaching of empowerment says that God loves all of us equally and unconditionally, now and for all time. God's love is steady and all-inclusive. It is the very foundation of our existence.

Once given, it cannot be taken away. If we don't feel this love, it is not because God has stopped loving us. It is because we have cut ourselves off from the awareness of God's love. This is not God's predicament, but ours.

The teaching of vicarious atonement says that God and Jesus have an enemy whose name is Satan. Satan is an independent agent for evil, a kind of God run amuck, the black sheep in the celestial family. Satan tempts us and leads us astray.

The teaching of empowerment says that God has no opposite or enemy. There is no devil who can become the scapegoat. No one else is to blame for the choices that we make.

The teaching of vicarious atonement says that it is okay to kill as long as God is on your side. God himself sacrificed his only begotten Son on the cross and asked Abraham to sacrifice Isaac.

The teaching of empowerment says that there is never any justification for murder or abuse.

These are different world views. Each results in a certain set of values and beliefs.

The teaching of vicarious atonement says that human beings

are sinners. Left to their own inclinations/devices, they will continue to sin. Their only hope is to be saved by Jesus.

The teaching of empowerment says that human beings are born innocent. If they are loved and respected, they will usually grow up to be loving, respectful human beings.

In the end, love is the only answer to the problems of human suffering.

The teachings of vicarious atonement assign the responsibility for all the good and evil that happens *outside of ourselves.* Jesus saves us. The devil tempts us. We are but pawns in a struggle between good and evil.

The teachings of empowerment assign responsibility to us for the choices that we make. We are responsible for everything that we think, everything that we say, and everything that we do. There is no savior or tempter we can blame or hold responsible for the choices we make.

These are very different world views.

If you believe humans must be saved, your life becomes a quest to "save" others. You believe that you have the truth and know what's best for others.

So you preach, and shame, and cajole, not understanding that you are trespassing against others, not respecting their freedom to have their own beliefs and experiences.

On the other hand, if you understand that no one else can save you, and that you cannot save anyone else, you maintain appropriate boundaries. You respect the beliefs and experiences of others even when you don't agree with them. You don't try to make decisions for others or allow others to make decisions for you.

"No one can serve two masters."
(MATTHEW 6:24)

You cannot serve both of these teachings. You serve one or you serve the other.

If you serve the teachings of vicarious atonement, you accept the gospels as they have come down to us as the absolute word of God and you interpret them literally.

You don't believe that the Master's teachings can be clarified or adapted to today's needs through direct communion with him. You do not accept the authority of present-day revelation.

If you serve the teachings of empowerment, you find guidance and inspiration not only in the gospels, but in your direct communion with Jesus in your heart of hearts. For you, revelation is an on-going reality in which guidance and insight are received.

In the former case, the Book is closed. Everything has already been said.

In the latter case, the Book is open and must remain open if the teaching of the Master is to be renewed and received fully by people in each generation.

The teachings of vicarious atonement run hand in hand with religious fundamentalism. For fundamentalists, the Word is truth and every word is to be studied, dissected, and interpreted. Fundamentalists affirm an outer or external authority.

On the other hand, the teachings of empowerment run hand in hand with mystical experience.

Mystics trust their direct experience of the divine as much, if not more, than the words of scripture. They affirm an inner or internal authority.

Ironically, Bibles and scriptures document the mystical experiences and revelations of the past. They are helpful in this respect.

However, when they become a straightjacket and cause people to doubt the validity of their own experience, they become dogmatic and counterproductive.

Faith requires an element of experience and a dialog with the divine, for you cannot have faith in something that you have not experienced.

Faith and mystical experience are inevitably intertwined.

When you take away the experience of God, the belief in God becomes narrow, predictable and blind.

It was into such a time that Jesus was born. The Judaism of his time was pale, vapid, and musty. It lacked energy and life. It lacked the passion and conviction of experience.

Today, Christianity finds itself in the same boat.

The time for a renewal of the faith has come. If you are reading these words, you understand that this is necessary for you and for many others.

People often say to me, "I cannot accept the teachings of the Church, but I still love Jesus. I still feel that he is my teacher."

If this is you, take heart. Wipe away the preconceptions of the past and come to him with empty hands. He will teach you. He will guide you.

He simply awaits your invitation.

"The Kingdom of God is within you."
(LUKE 17:21)

God's authority is not outside. It is not in the world. It is not in the words and beliefs of other men and women.

It is in your heart of hearts.

Once you call God into your heart, your life changes forever. For that is when you reject an external authority and claim an internal one.

You are walking now in the footsteps of the Master, who like all prophets, experienced guidance and spiritual revelation through direct communion with God.

Now you, like him, have become a heretic and an anathema to all religious hierarchies. Now you run the risk of being excommunicated, cast out of the fold, just as he was.

Clergy may become angry at you because you do not submit to their authority, because you refuse to be controlled by them or to play by their rules.

They may be threatened by you, fearing that others will emulate you and challenge their ecclesiastical power, privilege and authority.

It is no different now than it was in Jesus' time. Now the Pharisee simply wears a Christian robe. Now the priest or bishop is the wolf dressed up in sheep's clothing. And he will do everything he can to silence you so that his sins can be buried from sight.

Now you have the same choice Jesus had—to betray yourself and your faith—or to stand up for the truth you hear in your heart and for your right to decide what is true for you and what is not.

"Their teachings are but rules taught by men."
(MATTHEW 15:9)

Jesus refused to be controlled by liars and hypocrites who distorted the scriptures and made up their own rules to benefit themselves and to shame and discredit others who would challenge their judgment or authority.

It is a sad fact that only the weak and the insecure seek to dominate and control others. Yet this is the legacy not just of kings and dictators, but also of all clergy who wield secular power, no matter how cleverly it is disguised in the cloak of religion.

It is the story of those who terrorize others in the name of God (who has many names) or in the name of Jesus or any other savior or prophet.

The time has come for organized religion to clean up its act. It is time for evangelists from all traditions to call off and condemn the holy wars. For no God or spiritual master condones any form of violence or persecution.

It is time for the citizens of planet earth to be done with the culture of violence. This is the heartfelt urging of all spiritual masters from all of the great traditions.

It is time to reject the language of hatred and intolerance that divides and fragments the human community and to embrace a new language of tolerance and love.

It is time to reject the teachings of fear and let the Spirit of love be reborn in our homes, our communities and our places of worship.

"I am the Light of the World."
(JOHN 8:12)

Jesus was a wayshower. He showed us how to shine our light.

If we love Jesus, it is our greatest desire to emulate him, to have the courage to speak the truth, even when the truth is not popular.

This is how the light continues to shine in the darkness.

Following Jesus means having the courage to challenge every form of inequality and every instance of betrayal or abuse of human rights and human dignity.

You do not do this to be provocative, self-righteous, or to humiliate those who offend. You do this to protect the innocent, not to condemn the guilty.

It is never acceptable to shame or ridicule others. You cannot call for love in an unloving way and be following the example of the Master.

What you say and how you say it, what you do and how you do it, the means and the ends must be congruent.

That is why it is not easy to stand for truth. If you attack another, you are not standing for truth, but merely standing against him.

That is not truth. That is spiritual pride.

To stand for truth, you must hold the other in your heart and speak to him kindly and in a heartfelt way.

This is the language of love.

When others are spoken to in this way, their hearts open to you and to the words that you speak.

This is a radical teaching

It is not for those who need to play it safe, nor is it for those who seek the limelight at the expense of others.

This is not a teaching that puts anyone down or that feeds anyone's ego. It is not a teaching for those who need to be right or need to make others wrong.

This is a teaching that asks us to honor every human being without exception.

It is a teaching that asks us to be strong without trespassing on others, to be gentle and accommodating without inviting the trespass of others.

It is a teaching of absolute, uncompromising equality.

It is not hard to understand, but it is very challenging to practice, for it asks us to look at every judgment we make about ourselves or others.

It is not surprising that few human beings have chosen to walk fully on this path, for it is a path that requires great clarity and strength.

But the time will come when more will be called to do this work, for the survival of human consciousness and its next evolutionary step will require it

3

Knowing God

MAKE NO GRAVEN IMAGES

One of the cornerstones of Jewish thinking is the understanding that God is always larger than we think He is. He just doesn't fit inside our definitions. Words cannot do justice to Him.

In Judaism there is a certain healthy distance between God and His creation. This distance helps us stay humble and continue to feel reverence and awe for the divine, which is ever beyond our grasp.

The danger here is that the distance at times becomes too great. The human feels unworthy and God becomes unapproachable.

The Gnostic's answer to this problem was to locate God not outside, but inside human consciousness itself.

This was not an idea that was foreign to Jesus.

Yet the Gnostic approach creates the potential for distortion at the opposite pole.

While the inscrutable God becomes distant and inaccessible, restricting our capacity for intimacy with the divine, the God within consciousness can become too easy to find, thereby trivializing our relationship with Him and with the deeper aspects of our own consciousness.

Gnosticism invites us to have an ongoing dialog with the divine, but it runs the risk of limiting God to our past understanding and experience.

Christ offers a synthesis of these two ideas, for he is human and we can know him intimately, yet he is also divine and beyond our everyday knowledge and experience. We can have a relationship with Christ, but not through our ego structure.

To know Christ, our consciousness must shift and expand.

Our hearts and minds must open to new levels of understanding and compassion.

That means that we can encounter spiritual truth within our own consciousness but, to do so, we will have to transcend our fear-based, reactive thinking patterns and the behavior associated with them. To know God, we must heal our deepest wounds and move beyond the need to be a victim or a victimizer.

HEALING OUR WOUNDS

To be wounded then does not totally cut us off from God. It just tells us that we cannot feel God's love in our wounded state.

We must do our emotional healing work first so that we can begin to experience our wholeness. For it is only in our wholeness that we can experience God's unconditional love for us.

We become whole in Christ because Christ is the one who has healed, the one who has forgiven himself and others. Christ consciousness is a transitional state in the journey from the human to the divine.

Before we enter that state, we appear to be separate from God and from each other. After we enter it, we know there is no separation. We know that we humans are essentially equal and each of us lives and abides in the unconditional love and acceptance of God.

Awareness of this Oneness is the radical understanding that Jesus embodies.

We can know God without limiting Him.

We do not have to limit God to our present understanding. Each day we can surrender our concepts of God and come to Him with empty hands.

We can know ourselves and others in the same way. Indeed, this is how we cultivate humility. We recognize the limits of what we know and become willing to move beyond them.

Knowing God is not a single, static event. It is an unfolding experience. The more we surrender what we think we know, the more we open to what we do not yet understand.

That is why we empty our cup before approaching the altar. We make room for a new understanding. We open to new insight, new revelation.

We reclaim our innocence in each moment. We become a blank slate for God to write on. How do you think that Moses received the *Ten Commandments?* How do you think Jesus was given the *Sermon on the Mount?*

All the prophets learned to approach God in this reverential yet intimate manner. That is what "awe of God" means. We never minimize the greatness of God, nor do we fall into the conceit or mistaken belief that we know who God is and what He wants from us. Instead, we come to Him as little children. We come to Him empty-handed and ask, "Father, What is your will for me today?"

The prophets were men and women who made the space to listen to God and brought us their understandings. None of them were perfect, but each had an expanded consciousness and a willingness to seek the truth beyond the limits of his ego structure.

And, if we desire to grow spiritually, we must do the same. We must never be content with the little that we understand. We must never be satisfied by putting God into a conceptual box and leaving Him there. For, if we do, it will not be God that we see, but the narrow structure of our own beliefs.

Jesus represented the flowering of the prophetic tradition. For he brought through not just a moral teaching, but evidence of a relationship with God that anyone could ask for and receive. And it is through that relationship that we receive new information and learn to let go of our biases and prejudices.

If we are willing, God will teach us. If we are willing to surrender our error and misconception, He will correct us and set us onto the right path. He does this not just by sending us His teachers and prophets. He does it by entering into direct dialog and communion with us in our hearts.

If this dialog and communion were not possible, there would be no present-day revelation. There would be no way for us to correct our misunderstandings of God and to go beyond our limited perceptions of Him. And there would be no way for us to correct our misperceptions of ourselves or of our brothers and sisters.

If a direct relationship with God were not available, all we would have is what has already been written or said about God. We would be limited to the perceptions of the scribes who wrote the teaching down and the preachers who interpret it.

But Jesus made it clear that such a relationship was possible. Indeed, he called us to it.

He asked us to listen to God in the silence of our hearts. For that is where we would be able to discriminate between truth and falsehood, regardless of the source. There we would know the difference between right and wrong, truth and illusion.

All bibles, scriptures, holy books and all new revelatory material must pass through the silence of the heart where their degree of helpfulness to us will be made clear. That which is helpful will resonate and ring true. And that which is not helpful will feel hollow and out of harmony with our soul.

Communion with God is a hallowed act. In this act of communion, we come to know God's will for us. We do not, and cannot know God's will for anyone else. Only s/he can know it by entering into direct communion with the divine.

Each one of us is responsible for what we believe and what we accept into our hearts and minds. That is because we were given by God the power to choose. So let us exercise it well. Let us choose only that which resonates with us heart and soul. For anything else is not worthy of us, nor able to guide us through the hills and valleys of our human experience.

Christ has no need of bibles or scriptures.
Love is his gospel.

Because he lives in direct communion with God, Christ has no need of bibles, scriptures, or moral codes. He is the living truth and all that he does is done in love and harmony.

Christ does not pause to consider whether to condemn or to bless, attack or forgive, criticize or comfort. He is the embodiment of all that encourages and supports.

Acts of cruelty cannot come from him. He cannot hurt his brother, for he knows that to hurt another is to hurt himself.

Equality is not just an idea for him. It is the living truth.

And he witnesses to it in the face of injustice and inequity.

His is not just a gospel of love. Love is his gospel. It is his legacy, told not merely in words but in actions that speak louder than words.

Those who were touched by him remember how he touched them, how he looked at them as if he was seeing into the essence of their souls, and how he helped to uplift their hearts from the burdens of doubt and fear.

A master like Jesus doesn't teach from a book. He quotes the book only because you value it.

The master reinforces truth wherever he finds it. His walk and talk weave together seamlessly. That is why the people say "There goes Jesus. Let us go and sit with him."

When you find where your treasure is and live from that place, you will not need to quote scripture or read truth from books written by others, you will speak the words that are given to you as they are given. For you, like your teacher, will become a mouthpiece for truth.

Your choice will be merely whether or not to open your mouth and let the words come out. You will not be able to stop the words from coming into your ears.

Yet before you can consider whether to say yes or no to God, His Spirit will enter into you and His words will be sounded through your lips. You may or you may not remember the words that you speak, but others will remember them and come to Him through you.

All this will be beyond your understanding or control. It is the power of Spirit at work in the world. Had you not volunteered for the assignment, had you not told God that you were ready and willing to serve, none of this would happen.

So before you call God into your life, think twice. Right now, your life belongs to you. When you invite God in, your life will belong to Him.

Jesus was more than willing to make that offer to God. You must make your own choice.

AND THE TRUTH SHALL SET YOU FREE

Many have asked "how do I know truth when I encounter it?" It is not difficult to recognize spiritual truth if you understand that it is not just apprehended by the mind. It is also felt in the heart and in the body.

A true statement "rings true." It establishes a vibratory sensation that you can feel. That is why we say "this feels right."

The teachings of love are not just words. They carry a spiritual energy that we may experience as a warmth in our heart, a ringing in our ears, a tingling in our hands or feet, or as energy going to other parts of our body.

Each person is activated by this spiritual energy in a unique way.

Let the way that you are activated be honored as a sign from God. It is the way that God says to you "Listen to this please" or "Pay attention; this is important."

ENTERING THE TEMPLE OF THE HEART

When your mind and heart are at peace, you are sensitive to the truth and can discern it easily.

When your mind is divided or distracted and you are emotionally triggered or upset, it is nearly impossible for you to discern truth or feel the energetic presence of love in your life.

This leads to a simple but important awareness.

When you wish to commune with God or Truth, you must withdraw from the drama of life and go into the inner sanctuary. There you begin to breathe, relax, surrender your thoughts and feelings and establish a vibration of love and trust in your heart and your mind.

That vibration is the gateway to the inner temple. It is here that you go to meet God, to feel His love and to hear His guidance.

The temple is not a physical place, but a psychological place, a place of peace, rest, nurturing, acceptance and love.

The temple does not come to you. You must go to the temple. You must shift your consciousness from agitation to peace, from fear to love. When you do that, you dwell with God and you can feel His presence and His love for you.

This is the core practice of both Judaism and Christianity. It is a daily practice. At least once each day you are to spend time in communion with God through your spiritual essence.

At least once per day, you are asked to leave the world behind and enter the inner sanctuary.

Lest you make time for God in this way, how can you understand His will for you and feel His love and His presence as you walk through life?

The time that you give to God is given also to yourself.

Indeed there is no greater gift that you can give to yourself or to anyone else than time you spend in communion with God in the silence of your heart.

Jesus told us "Love the Lord your God with all your heart and with all your soul and with all your mind. This is the first and greatest commandment." (Matthew 22:37-38)

Every day, in the course of living, the mind is distracted and heart is disturbed. That is why throughout the day, we must learn to take a deep breath, put aside our worries and fears, and clear out a space for God

That is why Jesus reminded us, "Man does not live on bread alone, but on every word that comes from the mouth of God." (Matthew 4:4; Deuteronomy 8:3)

This is the true bread of life. This is the real communion.

4

Serving God

DISCIPLESHIP

When we decide to follow the Word of God that we hear in our hearts, we accept what God wills for us. We cease to listen to the demands of our ego or anyone else's.

We are empowered by Spirit to live the life we came here to live. We step confidently into our life not because we are confident in ourselves but because we are confident in the One who sends us.

We know that we are not the ones who will accomplish the great works that are given us to do, but God will do these works through us. Our job is just to show up, to be fully present. God will give us the words to say. He will tell us how to act in the moment.

This takes a lot of pressure off of us. When we see the demonstration of God's power manifesting through us, we learn to trust it. We surrender. We submit to the inner authority of God expressing through our heads, hearts and hands.

We do not question it. We know that God knows more than we know and sees more than we see.

We have the little picture. He has the big one.

We know how our own little piece fits with the pieces beside us. God knows how all the puzzle pieces fit together because He has the consciousness of the whole.

He is All that is. He is all of the pieces, not in their separateness, but in their oneness.

When we are in communion with God, we too have the consciousness of All.

This is called Christ Consciousness. Our oneness with All enables us to be one with all expressions of God.

This is how equality—one of the great spiritual principles—is established in our consciousness and demonstrated on earth. It is the natural result of our relationship with God. It is the natural expression of Christ.

For Christ would not be Christ if he were not one with all of his brothers and sisters.

SERVICE IS THE GOAL OF SURRENDER

There would be no reason to surrender the ego if we were not called to a life of service. The transcendence of selfish agendas enables us to serve.

Until we learn to hold it gently, we cannot relinquish the ego, and we cannot serve until we let the ego go.

Ego is the belief that we are separate, and that we need to compete with others in order to survive. Its survival tactics are designed to meet our needs at the expense of others.

Our ego keeps us locked in our unworthiness. It reinforces our mutual trespasses and our victimization of self and others.

Ego consciousness and the beliefs attached to it are the great illusion. They create most of the suffering in our lives.

The paradox is that if you condemn the ego, it just gets stronger. It is tenacious, like a wisteria vine that chokes the tree it encircles.

You cannot relinquish the ego with the ego. It does not work. That is why Jesus told us "Resist not Evil."

The ego can be relinquished only by love and acceptance. When you love and accept your ego, it loses its ground of being. Eventually, it ceases to exist. It dissolves in the love that holds it.

The ego seems to oppose love, but it cannot really do so. Love has no opposite. It is all-inclusive. Everything that we bring into the circle of love is transmuted by that love.

As we learn to hold all our states of consciousness in a loving way, we become more considerate and forgiving of others. We learn to bless instead of condemn. We become less reactive to our own fear and the fear of others.

Love places us into service by bringing into our lives the people who need our love and are ready to receive it.

That is when our ministry becomes clear.

SELF-NOMINATION

By understanding the call of God in your heart, trusting it and following it where it leads, you nominate yourself to serve. This is your side of the covenant with the divine.

First you must be willing. Then you must be ready.

If you are ready, you are immediately placed into service. If you are not ready, your training begins. You attract experiences that teach you, open your heart to love's presence, and increase your vibration.

As you connect more readily with love, you naturally relinquish your need to rely on your ego to function in life.

Whereas before you needed to plan everything, now you are

able to be present in the moment and be open to what comes. As a servant of God, your mind remains flexible and alert and your heart remains open.

At any moment, often without warning, you may be called upon to speak or to act. In this way, your willingness is continuously tested.

The more you trust your divine guidance, the more God entrusts you with His work here. You become the light in the darkness, the voice in the wilderness.

You are the one He sends to offer healing to those in pain, sanctuary to those who are persecuted, acceptance and love to those who have been rejected or judged unworthy.

As a servant of God, you are placed in the world to heal the sick, tend the needy, and uplift those who despair. Because of you, the light of God is visible in the darkest moments, and the love of God remains palpable in the midst of loss or grief.

While you nominate yourself for service, it is God who ordains you. No human being can do this, for no human being knows who you are, why you are here, or who will come to you to be healed.

Even you do not fully know this. Yet when you surrender to the divine, your gifts are gradually revealed.

They emerge as you answer the call and flower as you learn to give them freely and unconditionally to all who ask for them.

PERFECTION

The greatest impediment to service is the belief that we must be perfect to serve God.

No one is perfect. Even Jesus was not perfect, but he was willing to trust God's guidance, and we can do the same.

It is through our relationship with God that we are purified and given the strength and the wisdom to serve.

Do not let false humility or unworthiness hold you back from making a commitment to your spiritual life.

Your willingness is what matters. If you are willing, God will do the rest. He will teach you and guide you. He will steady your heart, open your mind, and use your gifts to help others.

You may not believe that you have any gifts to give. But it does not matter. Simply tell him: "Lord, I place whatever gifts and talents I may have in your hands. Please use them as you see fit."

Serving God requires genuine humility. You must realize the limits of what you know and be willing to learn. But it does not require false humility.

Shame and unworthiness only prevent you from coming into your full power and purpose. Do not let them stand in your way. Instead pray these words: "Lord, let this burden be lifted that I might step into my power and purpose and serve the greater good."

The world does not benefit if you live a timid life bent on sacrifice. It benefits from your strength, not your weakness.

"But I feel weak," you say. Then give that weakness to God and ask for the courage to trust and to risk.

Do not hide. Do not hold back. Do not shy away. The world needs your love. Your spouse needs your love. Your children need your love. You need your love.

A life without love is a life without dignity or purpose. It is not worth living. That is why many people feel depressed or even suicidal. They have nothing to live for. They pull into themselves. They inhabit their own inner darkness, unaware of the spiritual light.

Do not settle for such a life. Kindle the Godlight within. Pray into it. Love into it. Love yourself, your family, your friends. Be kind and loving even to strangers. And you will feel the inner spark rise into a flame. Your heart will dance and hope and faith will return.

GOD'S ETERNAL LOVE

God holds you always in His heart. This you must know and, if you do not know it, this is what you must learn.

God loves you as you are. He does not ask you to be better or wiser than you are.

He does not want you to be like anyone else. God accepts and loves you without conditions. God says: "I love you, son or daughter. Be assured of that love and know that I am with you."

If you do not have this awareness of the divine, you must cultivate it. You must enter the inner temple at least once every day. Do so not to ask for favors or material things, but ask to feel His love in the depths of your heart.

It is that unconditional and all embracing love that will sustain you throughout the day. It is for this that you pray: "Lord I ask for your presence in my life today. May I feel your love and know that you are with me in all that I think, all that I say and all that I do."

Begin your day with this prayer and repeat it throughout the day. This is how you will come to know God.

Because you ask, He will come. Because you make a place in your heart for Him, He will abide with you.

Because you ask for His help, He will guide you. He will be with you because you have taken the time to be with Him, for that too is your covenant with Him.

Your relationship with God asks something not just from Him. It asks something from you too.

It is not a one-way relationship.

Even though He is always there for you, you cannot feel His presence except when you ask for it. If you don't show up, if you don't ask, God cannot make Himself known to you.

For knowing Him and being with Him are one and the same. You cannot know God without being present with Him.

That is why we take time for meditation, contemplation and prayer. That is why every day and, as necessary throughout the day, we invite God into our minds and our hearts.

St. Francis prayed, "Lord, Make me an Instrument of Your Peace."

We cannot be an instrument of God's peace if we don't take the time to experience that peace. We must experience peace first in our own hearts if we are going to be able to extend it to others.

Those who try to heal before they have been healed are unhealed healers. They bring nothing but trouble to themselves and to others.

You cannot give what you do not have.

Do not be like Don Quixote riding out on your white horse to try and save the world. Save yourself first. Establish the kingdom first in your own heart, and it will automatically extend to others.

Then, wherever you go, the love of God will go with you and others will feel it and be drawn to you. This is the law of attraction. People are drawn to the vibration of love because love is what they want.

Of course, this has nothing to do with you as a personality or as an ego. It has to do with the love that you embody. You are just an instrument. It is not the instrument that matters but the music that emanates from it. It is not you, or me, or St. Francis, or even Jesus that matters. It is the love that we embody.

Christ is the expression of God's love in the world. It is the living presence here among us. It is the hands and the feet of God. It is the voice of God. It is the will of God made manifest through us.

So we must be humble. We must give the credit to God. We are not the ones who heal or uplift. It is the Spirit of God that moves through us that heals and uplifts.

You cannot serve God and feed your ego. You cannot be narrow or selfish and express the love of God.

What the ego needs and what God needs are totally different. The ego needs appreciation, approval, praise, recognition, fame, and glory. It needs to be pumped up because it does not know its true value.

God needs none of these things nor does the core self, the essence in all of us that is connected to God. The core self is the pure instrument. It is content to be the expression of the divine in each moment.

It needs no recognition or approval. It delights in transmitting love, for it understands that to give love is to receive it. Therefore giving is an act of bliss and a continual blessing to both self and other.

To rest in the core self is to reinforce core self in others. To embody love is to awaken the connection to love in the hearts of others.

That is why the instrument is needed. Not to call attention to itself, but to announce the ever-present reality of love.

That is the melody we hear and the rhythmic connection we feel in the presence of a spiritual master. She emanates pure love. She vibrates pure joy. She enfolds all beings in her unconditional acceptance. In her embrace, we feel peace. We feel connected to our core self and our Source.

GOD'S WILL FOR US

God's will for us is that we stand in our power, speak and live our truth, and help others to do the same. When we are aligned with our core self, God's will and our will are one and the same.

Only when we are aligned with our ego (when we think our fears are real), does our will and God's will seem to conflict. As in all instances of conflict, the way to peace and reconciliation is to bring love and acceptance.

Let us accept our ego needs without identifying with them. Let us watch our fear rising and see how it results in all kinds of self-limitation, unhappiness, victimization and scarcity thinking. Let us see all this without buying into it. Let us see and hear all of it simply as a call for love. And then let us bring compassion to the wounded child within us who is in fear, assuring him/her of our love.

That will bring a shift to a deeper level of consciousness. It will help us move from fear/anxiety to love/acceptance. It will re-connect us to our core self.

To bring love to ourselves is the most important act any of us can engage in. It is the essence of our spiritual work.

Only when we rest in the core self can our will and the will of our Creator join together as one.

Let us not be discouraged when separation from Self and from Source occurs. It will occur again and again.

Our goal is not to try to stop it from occurring, but to learn to find our way back to Oneness as efficiently as possible.

As soon as we see that we are "needing love," we know that it is our job to bring it. Each of us is the savior who brings love to our wounded child when it is needed.

When we learn to do this for ourselves, we can teach others to do it. But we cannot do it for them.

Salvation is an inside job. It happens within the heart and mind of each person.

5

Creating with God

CREATING WITH LOVE

When we create with awareness of our Source, we create with love and what we create blesses and multiplies. It helps us and it helps others. Love is abundant. There is no limit to how much love there is or how much it can do.

When we create without awareness of our Source, we create with fear and limitation. We believe that resources are in short supply and that we need to appropriate them before others do.

This is scarcity thinking. It leads to suffering.

When we take or monopolize resources that do not belong to us, we cannot enjoy them. We are ever afraid of losing what we have and spend a lot of time defending what we have selfishly gained.

The lesson is a clear one: There is no gain to be found in another's loss. Either both sides gain or neither side does.

KNOWING WHAT WE WANT

Caring and commitment are the essential ingredients of success in the manifestation of our desires.

If we are ambivalent, if we don't know what we want, or if we know what we want but are not fully committed to achieving it, we will not be successful.

The process of creation starts with knowing what you *do* want, not with knowing what you *don't* want. Knowing what you *don't* want can be helpful only if it leads you to knowing what you *do* want. Otherwise, it justifies complaining and reinforces your powerlessness.

The way to create peace is not to say "I don't want war," because then your focus is on war, not on peace. If you want to create peace, ask for peace. Get in touch with what peace looks and feels like. Get in touch with how much you desire it.

Once you know what you want, you must believe that it is possible to create it. You won't hit 50 home runs a year if you don't believe that you can. You won't create peace in your world if you don't believe you can.

CO-CREATING

If you want to know whether you and God are on the same page, ask "Is this for my highest good?"

If it is for your highest good, it will benefit others. If it will not benefit others, it may not be for your highest good.

When you begin to co-create with God, you won't be interested in manifesting cars, houses, yachts and private planes. You will be manifesting healing, peace, and enough food and shelter to feed the hungry and the homeless.

If you doubt this is possible, ask for a private audience with Mother Teresa.

The principle of creation is simple: the Source of healing, peace, abundance and everything else that we need in life is within consciousness itself.

We are all powerful beyond measure. This is what Jesus tried to tell us in the *Sermon on the Mount.*

LIVING IN DIALOG WITH GOD

When we know we are loved and accepted, we can be ourselves confidently, without apology.

When we do not know this, we struggle, make excuses, betray ourselves or others and find it difficult to show up.

People who know they are loved think and act differently from those who don't. They have a different relationship to themselves, to others, and to the universe.

People who know they are loved expect their prayers to be heard. They know that God's help is on the way, even though it may come in a form that is different from the one they expected.

They are willing to trust God, and they live feeling His support in their lives. Others find it easy to support them because they are hopeful and have a positive attitude.

On the other hand, people who feel inadequate, ashamed, broken, damaged or unworthy do not feel supported by God, by their families or by others. Their relationship to the universal supply is blocked by their beliefs about themselves and others.

When they pray, they do so out of a feeling of deprivation, perhaps even anger. They do not expect positive results. They expect to be disappointed. And so they are.

Even when their prayers are answered, they cannot recognize the gifts that have been offered because they expect them to come in a different package.

They do not live in a familial dialog with God and so God appears distant and detached and His actions seem arbitrary and unfair.

None of this is true, but it is what they believe and so it becomes true. It becomes a self-fulfilling prophecy.

CONSCIOUSNESS IS CREATIVE

Whatever you believe, you will create on some level and to some degree. That is because consciousness is creative.

Of course, you do not create in a vacuum or in a linear fashion. Others are also creating and their creations impact yours.

Nevertheless, the content of your consciousness does, more than anything else, tend to shape your experience of the world.

The outer life—the three dimensional world—tends to reflect the dominant beliefs and emotions held within consciousness.

That is why any meaningful change happens from the inside out. We have to shift those dominant beliefs and emotions if we want to have a different experience in the world.

Of course, most people focus on making changes to the outer form or circumstances of their lives. They change their physical address, change jobs, or change relationships. But this by itself does not work.

Only if there is a corresponding inner shift will outer changes hold up. Otherwise, in spite of outer attempts to change, consciousness will recreate the old conditions.

You can't make a lasting change in behavior without changing the consciousness that gives rise to it. This is why many addicts have trouble staying sober or clean. They address the symptom, not the cause.

On the other hand, when consciousness changes, external conditions are bound to follow suit, even if one is not pursing external change.

Form follows content. New wine requires new skins.

When we are committed to change within our hearts and minds, it manifests effortlessly in our world.

Whatever you have asked for in prayer, believe that you have received it and it will be yours."

(MARK 11:24)

If we want to understand how prayer works, we need to realize that God is not going to give us what we do not want or what we are not ready to receive.

He is not going to change the outer form if the contents of consciousness have not shifted.

So if we want something different on the outside, we must surrender our old, dysfunctional beliefs and the emotions we have invested in them.

If that is difficult, we can ask God for help. We can pray for the shift within, instead of asking for outer change, and we can vow to cooperate with the opportunities life provides us to change our minds and open our hearts.

This is part of our ongoing dialog with God. It is hard to ask God to do something for you if you are not willing to do your part.

Remember, a life lived in Spirit is a co-creation. It is a partnership with God.

God will give you what you really want, but you must get clear on what this is and know if it is for your highest good. Otherwise, you may get what you asked for, but you will not be happy with it.

Prayer is part of the co-creation process. It is a time to be honest with God and to ask for His help.

So let us come to prayer with a willingness to do our part in the process. We cannot ask for something new unless we are ready to surrender something old that no longer works in our lives.

When we are fully committed to the transformation of our consciousness, we know with a certainty that outer events and circumstances will shift to accommodate our change of mind and heart. We know that our prayers will be answered, and everything that we think, say or do is consistent with this understanding.

A Prayer of Gratitude

And so we pray:

Thank you God
for helping us to remember
the blessing you gave to us
in the moment of our Creation.

We celebrate the fact that this blessing
is as real now as it was then.

Nothing has changed.

We are your children
and as your children we abide
in the safe harbor of your love
now and for all time.

This is the gift eternal
from you to us.

And so it is.
Amen.

6

Healing with God

ATTENDING TO OUR WOUNDS

All human beings are wounded and all must take the time to heal. Pain is usually the wake up call that motivates us to pay attention to the wound and begin to bring love to it.

All healing merely consists of bringing love to a part of ourselves that does not feel loved or loveable. And, of course, the love that is required is unconditional love, not conditional love.

Unconditional love is based on acceptance. We accept the wound because it is there and it is asking for our attention. If we deny the wound, it cannot heal.

Bringing attention, awareness, acceptance, love and compassion to the wound is the first step in healing.

The wound has many layers. If we keep peeling back the layers, we begin to realize that the ultimate wound is self-betrayal and the refusal to love and accept ourselves.

The wound may seem to be about others abandoning us, betraying us or attacking us, and we must accept that as the doorway into healing. However, when we walk through the door, we begin to realize that this has nothing to do with anybody else.

All of this is about our relationship with ourselves. It is all about coming to love and accept ourselves unconditionally just as we are. As we bring love and acceptance to ourselves, the wound begins to heal.

In the end, when we rest inside the blessing of our self-acceptance and love of self, we realize that the wound itself is an illusion. When love is fully present, the wound cannot exist.

It is ironic perhaps that we have to feel pain to address a

wound that is ultimately unreal. Yet pain is the doorway from untruth to truth, from illusion to reality. And the healing agent that enables us to pass through that door is always love.

In our love and acceptance of ourselves, healing is possible, not just for us, but for the world that we live in. For in loving ourselves, we become a beacon of light and a force for healing in the world.

FORGIVENESS

Forgiveness is a way of bringing acceptance and love to ourselves and others. It is an essential aspect of the healing process.

When we refuse to forgive, we cannot heal. Instead, we hold on to the wound. We hold on to grievances against others or to shame and guilt for our own actions. Either way, we establish an identity in being wounded.

The forgiveness process starts with accepting what happened and processing all the feelings associated with it. If we process deeply and fully, we will encounter our unworthiness, our self-hatred and our rage toward others. We will bring all this into our conscious awareness.

It is a courageous act to bring this unconscious material up into the light. We take the torch of awareness and enter the catacombs of the soul to see all the brokenness, all the shame, all the personifications and projections of fear. By doing so, we proclaim that they will not remain hidden from sight any longer. They will be brought into the light, understood, accepted, loved and ultimately integrated. In this way, the inner dragons are tamed and their energy can be focused in a constructive way.

Many people think that forgiveness is about forgiving others. That is just the beginning of the process. True, deep, transformational forgiveness is about forgiving ourselves, not about forgiving others.

Forgiveness is part of an atonement process. It enables us to move from fear to love, from shame to acceptance, from isolation to connection, and from separation to oneness. When we atone, we come back into harmony with our core self, with others, and with God.

By forgiving ourselves, we take responsibility for loving ourselves. We stop blaming others and instead look at our own thoughts, feelings and actions. We see how we attract certain experiences based on our beliefs about ourselves. By making those beliefs conscious, we see how they drive our experience and we realize that this does not need to continue. Our awareness of our reactive patterns offers us the potential to make different choices.

TAKING PERSONAL RESPONSIBILITY

Our growth on the spiritual path requires that we learn to take responsibility for all that we think, say and do. That means that we are willing to admit our mistakes and atone for them.

We atone in two important ways. We ask for forgiveness from anyone we have hurt and we promise to learn from our mistakes so that we do not repeat them.

We can also offer to offset the effects of our errors by making some kind of restitution or by taking on some of the burdens of those we have injured or hurt.

All of this must be done in a heartfelt manner or it means very little. If we feel anything less than genuine remorse for our actions, our attempts to atone will not be successful. They will not release us from guilt.

TAKING COLLECTIVE RESPONSIBILITY

The advanced spiritual student learns to accept responsibility not only for his own actions but also for the actions of others. In this sense, he is responsible for everything that happens to him, good or bad.

Indeed, he is responsible for everything that comes into his field of awareness. So that if he is aware of a war, or a rape, or a murder, or any other kind of injustice, he becomes to some degree responsible for it.

Needless to say, there are not many spiritual students anxious to accept this level of responsibility. Yet Jesus told us clearly that we are our brother's keeper. We are responsible not just for what happens to us, but also for what happens for him.

Thus, we cannot turn a blind eye to any hurt or injustice, but must stand for equality and justice in every situation and at all times. This is what it means to take total responsibility.

"You have heard that it was said, Love your neighbor and hate your enemy. But I tell you: Love your enemies and pray for those who persecute you."
(MATTHEW 5:43-44)

When we are fully committed to love, we are committed to love all people, not just the people we like or agree with.

When we are fully committed to love, we are ready to love in every moment, not just when it is convenient for us.

It is because of this that Jesus could love and forgive those who crucified him. Although many people persecuted him, Jesus refused to cast them out of his heart. He practiced what he preached ("Love your enemies") and it was the depth and totality of his love and compassion that made Jesus a pure instrument for healing.

Since he condemned no one and loved without exception, he was in communion with the essence of all whom he met. Jesus was not distracted by the persona of others. He saw beneath the mask to the True Self.

He held the truth about people in his mind and brought them into his heart, affirming their worthiness to receive love. And, as he reached out his hands to bless and to heal, the power of the Holy Spirit moved through him.

Jesus knew that healing did not come from him. It came through him. Because his heart was open and his mind was clear, because he was willing to be a channel for love, God could work through him.

Jesus showed us how to be an instrument for love, healing and forgiveness in this world. In his presence, miracles occurred.

God can work through you and me in the same way if we too are willing to love everyone in our consciousness and experience. Indeed, this is how our world will be healed, not from the outside in, but from the inside out.

All we need to remember is that everything that appears to exist outside us also exists as a condition within consciousness. The rapist, the murderer, the terrorist are within us, as well as outside us.

If we forgive them and ask for their forgiveness, if we refuse to turn away from them but bless them and offer them our love, we will not only create peace within our own hearts and minds, but we will eventually create peace within our world.

For the inner and the outer are connected. As it is within, so will it be without. As it is above, so will it be on earth.

This the master knows. This is what the mastery student is learning.

HEALING OUR HEARTS AND OUR WORLD

Each day we become aware of many acts of cruelty and many instances of suffering in the world. It is easy to go into fear and to feel powerless. But we are not powerless.

When any news or evidence is presented to us of some form of violence, suffering or dis-ease in ourselves or in our world and we feel fear rising up in us, we have a choice. We can amplify the fear in our own consciousness, or we can bring love.

Bringing love means feeling our worthiness and our innocence. It means inviting God's loving presence into our minds and our hearts. It means staying in the consciousness of love until it totally surrounds and permeates our awareness of the problem or condition.

At that moment, we are holding our fear with love. At that moment, the problem or condition barely exists.

Instead, there is just love.

Every day we are presented with tragic news. What do we do with this information? Do we allow it to depress us and to make us feel powerless?

Do we feel angry and hopeless and leave it at that? Or do we understand it as an invitation to heal our own consciousness, to bring love and forgiveness to ourselves and others.

The master knows that healing the world and healing our hearts is the same task.

The world has many problems, but none of them can be solved by a vengeful mind or a bitter heart.

If you are looking for a powerful spiritual discipline, practice love and forgiveness after you listen to the news or read the newspaper.

Do the same thing whenever you are presented with any other tragic or stressful conditions. Take them into your consciousness and transmute them to acceptance and love. That is how the world is redeemed: in and through your consciousness and mine.

SPIRITUAL HEALING

Very few people understand what spiritual healing is. Spiritual healing does not involve fixing anything or anyone.

Spiritual healing merely corrects the misperception that there is something wrong. It affirms what is right and true under all circumstances and conditions.

Spiritual healing affirms the essential innocence of all beings. It affirms that all beings are worthy of love and acceptance. It affirms that all beings are equal before God and that no one is more or less worthy than anyone else.

The spiritual healer begins by bringing these truths into her consciousness and knowing them with a certainty. She affirms that the person who has requested healing is whole and complete in God's eyes and cannot be otherwise. This is the *mental* or *third eye component* of the healing process.

Next the spiritual healer opens her heart to receive God's unconditional love and acceptance. She feels the intensity of that love in her heart and allows the warmth and vibration to extend from her heart to the heart of the person who has requested healing. Now she and that person abide together in the vibration of God's unconditional acceptance and love. This is the *emotional or heart chakra* component of the healing process.

Now the two are joined together in love and truth. At this time, the healer may be guided to speak words of truth. If so, they will be spoken spontaneously as the *throat chakra* begins to vibrate. The healer may also feel a surge of energy in the hands and offer hands-on healing if the person is receptive to it.

When the energy of unconditional love is fully embodied, the *crown chakra* opens, enfolding both in the angelic presence. Both are One now with God, the Source of all Being.

Resting in the certainty of God's love, no untruth or illusion can stand. All beliefs and wounds resulting from lack of love are consumed in the purifying fire of the Holy Spirit.

Now, only Love is real and nothing else exists.

Now, the spiritual healer's work is done. Illusion has been dispelled and only truth remains. The kingdom of heaven has been restored on earth

7

Spirit Embodied in the World

THE MIRACLE OF LOVE

A life lived in Spirit has a quiet, simple dignity. We appreciate the little things in our experience. We live moment by moment, breath by breath. We live not just to create, to achieve, to get things done, but also to receive, to be, to savor and celebrate life as it unfolds.

In this sense, everything that happens in our lives is part of a miraculous chain of events, the brilliance of which we don't often perceive until much later.

Great miracles were ascribed to Jesus and the conditions around his birth. We are told he was born of a virgin, that he had the power to heal any person or condition, and that he could even raise the dead.

Yet all he asked from us is that we love God with all of our mind and heart and that we love each other without conditions. He did not ask us to perform great miracles, to demonstrate or parade our spiritual powers. He asked us to live an honest life, to be true to ourselves and kind to others. This was the essence of his teaching. It was a teaching that he constantly modeled and that he also taught his disciples to model.

If you ask Jesus to describe the person who exemplifies his teaching, he will tell you simply: her mind and heart are open. She is willing to serve and to share with others as life asks her to. She is humble and trustworthy.

She does not call attention to herself or betray the trust or confidence of others. She lives a simple life, free of selfish desires. She does not pursue name, or fame, or riches, but seeks truth and wisdom above all.

She knows that all the good things of life are given by the

grace of God, and she is content and grateful for the resources given to her. When she receives more than she needs, she shares it with those whose needs are greater than hers. Her greatest joy is to use the gifts of God to feed, house, care for and uplift the people of God.

Hers is not a glamorous life, nor is it a life lived in retreat from the world. She lives in the world, but is not of the world. Her consciousness rests in the divine and her words and actions are a constant reminder of God's love and presence here among us.

FOLLOWING IN THE DISCIPLES' FOOTSTEPS

Those who have dedicated their lives to serving God and His people have left a living legacy. We would do well to follow in their footsteps.

However, let us not raise any of them too high up on a pedestal. They would not want us to. For they understand that the more distance we place between them and us, the less likely we are to step forward into our own life purpose.

Instead, they would have us see them as they were when they took their first steps—afraid, lacking confidence, questioning their ability and their worthiness to serve. They would have us view them, not as gods or goddesses, but as human beings with doubts and fears just like our own. And they would encourage us to be brave and take risks, and not to underestimate our value or the value of the gifts that will be placed in our hands and given to others through us.

They would not have us be in awe of them or of what they have done. They would not have us overestimate their greatness, for in doing so we would only diminish our own and deny our gifts to those most in need of them.

This is an empowerment teaching. Those who walked in the footsteps of Jesus were empowered by Jesus to step into their purpose and be, as he was, the Servant of Love.

And they, in turn, would empower us.

Each of us lives not just for our own good and self-actualization, but also for the well-being and empowerment of others. Both light and love are meant to be shared. This is true in all spiritual teachings and traditions.

WITNESSING TO TRUTH

That is why discipleship is not an irrelevant issue, even today, when we must approach it with great caution and clarity.

To be a disciple is to be willing to be seen as a model and heard as a spokesperson for the teaching. A disciple should not preach or proselytize, for all beings must be encouraged to decide what is best for them and not take another's word or experience as truth for them.

A disciple knows that he does not have to twist arms to win hearts. He does not have to argue or convince others of the truth, for when they hear it they will know in their hearts and they will come gently into the fold.

The disciple knows that these matters of faith must be left to Spirit. If there is an argument to be made, it will be made by the voice of God within the heart and mind of the individual.

The teachings must be offered unconditionally to those who would listen to them and without strings attached. It is up to others to decide what speaks to their hearts and what does not. All attempts to interfere with the freedom of others to decide are simply trespass, no matter how cleverly they are disguised.

God asks each one of us to witness to our truth, to share with others what has helped in our own healing and empowerment. But He also asks us to be humble and restrained, to know that what works for us may not necessarily work for others.

Spiritual pride is one of the greatest obstacles on the path to illumination. We simply do not and cannot know what is for the highest good or is in the best interest of another human being, no matter how long or how deeply we have known him.

We do not know! Of course, he may not know either, but we must defer to him, for it his right to decide what to believe and how to live. That right is given to him by God and cannot be taken away from him by any woman or man.

There is no way that we can force another person to understand something he is not willing or ready to understand. Better to bite our tongue than to attack him with our words. Better to excuse ourselves and back away than to blindly persist and needlessly trespass on his freedom.

To witness is not to preach, not to advocate or condemn, but merely to offer our experience to others. Once we have done that, our work is done. We cannot be attached to the outcome. We must leave that to the Holy Spirit.

Lest we cultivate this respect for others and the restraint it requires, we cannot be a servant of the divine. Emotional investment in the choices that others make is a sign of our own weakness and insecurity. When we see we are attached to a certain outcome, or that we are inappropriately involved in the decisions of others, let us look to the inadequacy of our own faith, and not disguise it or seek to compensate for it by caring too much about what others do or leave undone.

Much of this is common sense. It simply requires a good sense of boundaries.

Yet organized religion, with its missionaries and messengers, does not score high marks on the litmus test measuring respect for the ideas and experiences of non-believers. The fact that Christianity is no exception to this rule is cause for scrutiny and concern. For if the followers of Jesus are not loving and respectful to others with whom they disagree, how can they call themselves Christians?

Let us be clear on this. What people call themselves is not necessarily what they are.

Jesus told us we would know the tree from its fruit. We need to remember that.

If the teaching of love is not taught in a loving way, it is not a teaching of love.

WORDS AND DEEDS

Words are powerful when they can be relied on.

A person who tells the truth, does what he says, and keeps his promises will be respected and held in high esteem. His advice and counsel will be sought.

On the other hand, a person who lies, misleads, and does not keep his promises will be distrusted and avoided.

Living a spiritual life requires us to tell the truth and keep our word. Honesty and sincerity are the compass that guide us.

A wise person does not make idle statements. He does not exaggerate, puff himself up or promise what he cannot deliver. He says very little at the beginning of a project but lets his hands, his feet and the sweat of his brow do the talking. He does not take money for work he has not done but collects his fee only when the task has been skillfully accomplished.

Humility is one of the greatest virtues on the path. When we walk our talk, we are naturally humble, for our words can be trusted and our deeds do not disappoint those who rely on them.

THE VALUE OF WORK

Spiritual mastery requires not just harmony in heart and mind, but skillfulness in the world, and the willingness to work and care for self, family, and community.

Sloth and laziness are major obstacles to spiritual growth. There is nothing spiritual in the behavior of a person who stalls, procrastinates or refuses to contribute his time, energy and attention to his own well-being and that of his community.

Each human being has the responsibility to care for himself and his family if he is able to. Society should not take that responsibility away, but encourage and prepare him to fulfill it.

Those who are called to a spiritual life are asked not only to take care of themselves and their families, but to care for and assist many others. Service to others is an integral aspect of their calling and commitment, for they are here to bring heaven to earth, to be God's hands and feet in the world.

AVOIDING EXTREMES

There are two extremes when it comes to work. One is workaholism (excessive/compulsive activity). The other is laziness or indolence (excessive passivity). In the former case, one is highly motivated and takes on too much responsibility. In the latter case, one is unmotivated and unable to take on even small responsibilities. Neither those who are driven to work nor those who are wary of work contribute to their well-being or that of others.

The spiritual life requires a balance between work and leisure, between doing and being. Too much work means not enough time to feed the soul. The result is a stressful life. Too little work means too many distractions for the mind and/or not enough resources to care for the body. The result is an aimless life, a life lived without dignity, self-confidence or a sense of purpose.

Those who are unemployed or living on trust funds will create balance in their lives by going to work and being productive. Those who are workaholics will create balance by taking time off from work to play, pray and decrease their levels of stress.

Living a spiritual life means taking the time not just to plant the roses, but also to smell them. If there is an imbalance here in your life, you would be wise to correct it without delay. For where there is awareness of truth, action must follow, or suffering intensifies.

FINDING THE BALANCE

A spiritual life requires finding balance between all extremes. It means not eating too much or too little. It means finding a healthy way of expressing our sexuality. It means finding a balance between being alone and being with others, between thinking and feeling, speaking and listening, doing and being.

Most of the so-called deadly sins are a result of excess or imbalance. Each one of us has, at one time or another, been guilty of committing one or more of the seven deadly sins. Yet each sin has a virtue that can be cultivated to bring balance back into one's consciousness and one's life. For example, the way to overcome *pride* is to cultivate *humility*, to realize the limits of what we know and to be willing to learn and to grow beyond our limits. The way to overcome *sloth* is to cultivate *diligence*, to be willing to show up when and where we are needed with energy and enthusiasm. The way to overcome *envy* is to celebrate the good fortune of others, to bless and to *praise* them for the gifts they bring and to pray for their continued success.

The way to overcome *anger* is to cultivate gentleness and *kindness* toward others and to undertake a sincere scrutiny of self to uncover our own wounds and to bring them to the light. The way to overcome *gluttony* is to practice *moderation*, and to inquire into the unworthiness and lack of self love that fuels our substance abuse or addiction. The way to overcome *greed* is to cultivate *generosity*, to share what we have with others and to refrain from taking more than we need so there are plenty of resources to go around. The way to overcome *lust* is to cultivate *intimacy*, and to channel our sexual energy so that we connect with our partners not just physically but on all levels.

96

8

Renewal of the Core Teaching

THE LAW AND THE SPIRIT OF THE LAW

Jesus came not just to uphold the Law but to embody the spirit behind it.

The *Ten Commandments* and the insights of the *Torah* are prescriptions for living, but if one follows them halfheartedly or just because one is afraid of the judgment of God or the rejection of one's community, one does not internalize the teaching or embody its spirit.

The first four commandments have to do with our relationship with God. They help us to understand and to cultivate that relationship.

The first commandment "You shall have no other Gods before me" tells us that God must come first in our lives. He is the highest of the high. Nothing else is more important than our relationship with him.

The second commandment exhorts us not to make or worship an idol, for all of our pictures of God are inadequate and can only trivialize our relationship with Him.

The third commandment tells us not to misuse the name of God. We must not take His name in vain or claim a relationship with Him we do not have.

The fourth commandment to observe the Sabbath asks us to set aside one day each week to remember God and to commune with Him.

Jesus combined these four commandments into one, summarizing them when he told us: "Love the Lord God with all your heart and with all your soul and with all your mind."

(Matthew 22:37, Luke 10:27) This he told us was the greatest of all commandments. That is because if our relationship with God is solid and reliable, our relationship with each other is bound to follow suit.

The next six commandments instruct us how we should treat each other. We are told to honor our parents, and exhorted not to murder, commit adultery, steal, lie or covet our neighbor's property. Jesus combined these six commandments into one, summarizing them when he told us, "Love thy neighbor as thyself." (Luke 10:27, Romans 13:9)

Jesus simplified the teaching not to water it down, but to make it easier for us to practice it. He took ten commandments and gave us two, but those two are more powerful than the ten because we can remember them easily and put them to work in our lives.

Jesus took the law and made it into a mantra that we could repeat throughout the day, thereby bringing the teaching more deeply into our hearts.

Love the Lord God with all your heart and all your soul and all your mind, and Love your Neighbor as Yourself.

This mantra is as powerful today as it was when Jesus gave it to us. I invite you to use it.

USING THE LORD'S PRAYER

The Lord's Prayer is a similar tool that Jesus gave us. It is easy to memorize and to repeat and it reinforces the same message.

Our Father Who Art in Heaven
Hallowed be Thy Name

This is the language of the Ten Commandments, only delivered not as prose but as poetry. God is the highest of the high and His name is holy. We have heard this before, have we not? But have we ever heard it more eloquently spoken?

Thy kingdom come,
Thy Will be done
on earth as it is in Heaven

More poetry. The Law of God is not to be found on some stone tablet of antiquity. It is here in our hearts. His will can be done here through us right now in this moment.

Indeed, we invite it to be done with these simple words.

Give us this day our daily bread
and forgive us our trespasses
as we forgive those
who trespass against us

Now we are moving on to commandments 6-10. We are asking God to provide for us so that we do not have struggle or take what does not belong to us.

If God is our source, we do not have to lie, steal, cheat or murder to survive. Perhaps we did not know before that our supply came from God so we trespassed on others.

So we ask now for forgiveness. We ask to be granted a clean slate, a new opportunity to practice the understanding we now have.

And in return we grant our brother and sister the same clemency so that s/he too may have the opportunity to live a life inspired by Spirit.

Lead us not into temptation, but deliver us from Evil (wrongdoing/illusion)

Of course, God never leads us astray. We are the ones who forget where our supply is, and we start to rely on our egos to create it, often at the expense of others. That is why we ask God to deliver us from our illusions so that we do not trespass against others and so ultimately do not injure ourselves.

For Thine is the kingdom, and the power and the glory, forever and ever.

And so The Lord's Prayer affirms our right relationship to God, to our brothers and sisters and to the world that we live in. Repeating it each day helps us to keep the *Ten Commandments* and to live in the spirit from which they came.

*"Do not think that I have come to abolish the LAW
or the Prophets; I have not come to abolish them
but to FULFILL them."*

(MATTHEW 5:17)

You do not understand Jesus if you think that he brought a new religion. He was a Jew speaking to Jews about Jewish law. Had the Jewish authorities accepted Jesus and his teaching, Judaism would have been renewed and it would have thrived in an unprecedented way.

It would have overcome its narrowness. It would have become a faith not just for a chosen people born to it by blood and familial ties, but a faith for all who wanted to live in an ecstatic relationship with God, a faith for all who were called to heal, to forgive, and to love.

A REBIRTH OF THE FAITH

Where Judaism found itself at the time of Jesus, Christianity finds itself today. It is time again for a renewal of the faith.

Narrowness must be transcended. Prejudices must be overcome.

The doors of the faith must be open to all people who would enter them. It does not matter what sex they are, or what sex their partner is. It does not matter what language they speak or what color skin they have. It does not matter what kind of car they drive or where they live.

No one must be barred from the doors to worship or leadership on any of these accounts.

The questions that we need to ask the one knocking on the door of the house of worship are not "How much money do you make?" and "What is your sexual preference?" They are "Is your heart open to the teaching of love as it has come down to us through Jesus and the other prophets?" and "Are you willing to do the work of emotional healing and transformation that will enable you to move out of fear and separation into a consciousness of acceptance and love?"

If they answer, "Yes," then they belong to the faith as much as you and I do. So let us not be the ones who try to block their entry or in any other way deny them the sanctuary God has promised them.

A faith that does not grow beyond its narrowness and its wounds cannot be renewed or reinvigorated. It cannot prosper, but will turn in upon itself, contract, and eventually die out.

It is because of this that new prophets and teachers arise in each generation, bringing the word in a fresh way, modeling the teaching for people facing the unique challenges of today.

Inevitably when a new prophet comes, the old guard is threatened, just as it was in Jesus' day. Yet the moment of truth arises and people will open their minds and their hearts or they won't. They will choose to awaken from illusion or to stay in the dream. The choices of yesterday and those of today are not as different as they seem.

"Now when he saw the crowds,
he went up on a mountainside
and he sat down. His disciples came to him,
and he began to teach them."

(MATTHEW 5:1-2)

The *Sermon on the Mount* is one of the great spiritual teachings of all time. In it Jesus gives us clear guidance about how we can live a spiritual life on earth.

In the *Beatitudes*, he tells us that we can be poor in our pocketbooks, yet still have great spiritual wealth. Indeed, he tells us that the poor are spiritually blessed and that the riches they receive from living a simple, modest life are far greater than any wealth the world could offer them.

He tells us that those who mourn will be comforted, for it is not a weakness to love nor is it a sin to grieve the loss of the beloved. He tells us that those who are gentle and kind will be given stewardship of the Earth. They will prevail over those who are ruthless, for the rule of Love will win over the rule of force and willingness will replace coercion.

Those who hunger and thirst for the truth will find it, he assures us, for truth eludes the grasp only of those who seek it half-heartedly. And those who are merciful will be shown mercy, for the actions of love multiply and always return to their place of origin.

The pure in heart will see God, he proclaims, even though wiser men and women may not, because God cannot be kept away from an open heart.

Blessed are they who are persecuted as the prophets were, he tells us, for those who know truth are never popular with those who have power and privilege.

He tells us not to be ashamed to suffer the indignities of the world for the sake of truth. Although the world will not reward us for our actions, they will not be forgotten, but will live in the ethers for all time. For the record of truth cannot be distorted or destroyed. It lives throughout eternity for all to see.

When Jesus spoke to the people from the mountaintop, he asked them to embody spiritual values in their lives. He told them *"Do not store up for yourselves treasures on earth, where moth and rust destroy, and where thieves break in and steal. But store up for yourselves treasures in heaven, where moth and rust do not destroy, and where thieves do not break in and steal. For where your treasure is, there your heart will be also.* (Matthew 6:19-21)

He told them (and he also tells us) that we cannot serve God and also serve money. We have a choice to make. If we choose to seek worldly rewards, we will squander the opportunities that we have in this life to wake up to our true Self. Jesus is so clear on this, it is impossible to misunderstand him.

How should we live then, if we are not to work for money or possessions? Are we asked to take a vow of poverty? Is it sinful to have more possessions than we need?

While he did not ask us to take a vow of poverty, Jesus is clear that having more than we need creates a spiritual burden. It consumes our time, energy and the focus of our consciousness. It also gives us the illusion that we are the Source and the one in control of our lives, when this is far from the case. The story of Job makes it clear to us that everything that we have can be taken away in a moment. It doesn't matter how good we have been or how skillful we are in managing our resources.

All of us are vulnerable to change and to shifts in fortune. Shifts like that threaten our ego structure and the very foundation of our lives. We have to have a spiritual framework to understand, accept and survive them. Most people at some point in their lives experience one or more of these kinds of changes in fortune. It could be a financial disaster, a divorce, the death of a child or a spouse, an addiction, a jail sentence, a near death experience, or a life-threatening illness.

Experiences like these are wake up calls. They tell us that it is time to stop wasting our time here on earth and get serious about why we are here and how we can make a contribution to the world that we live in.

Each of us comes here with a gift to give and a core wound to heal. The focus of our spiritual life must therefore be on healing our core wound and discovering our gift and learning how to give it.

When we commit to doing this with all our hearts and minds, there is a quintessential shift that takes place in our lives. We enter the great journey of healing and atonement that is helping human beings shift out of fear-based thinking into a consciousness of acceptance and love. At that time, God places us into service. That means that in return for our service, we trust God to provide for us and to put bread on our table.

We no longer rely on our own efforts, but trust in the power of love to be our perpetual supply. Of course, that does not mean that we are sitting around aimlessly waiting for God to make a delivery. We are out there moving our feet, giving our gift to all who ask for it, without worrying about the outcome. We trust that those who come to us do so because God is able to work through us to help them. And we trust that those who are able to assist us on all levels will be drawn into our lives.

That is what it means to live in trust, in faith and in surrender. That is the life that Jesus is talking about in the Sermon on the Mount. *"Look at the birds of the air,"* he tells us, *"they do not sow or reap or store away in barns, and yet your heavenly Father feeds them. Are you not much more valuable than they?"* (Matthew 6:26)

Jesus wants us to understand that God will take care of us if we will commit to be a Servant of Love and energetically move forward to heal our wounds and give our gifts.

Jesus is not asking us to live an ordinary life, but an extraordinary one. He is asking us to be "in the world, but not of the world." He is calling us to walk in his footsteps, to learn to trust God as he did, and thus to become spiritual masters.

The master does not worry about what he will eat, or drink, or wear. Like "the birds of the air," he knows that his needs will be met by life itself. He needs only to leave the nest and trust his wings.

All masters in training must remember well these important words: *"Seek first his kingdom and his righteousness, and all these things will be given to you as well."* (Matthew 6:33)

When we came into this embodiment, we were asked to learn to provide for ourselves and for our families. This was an important thing for us to learn to do. But there comes a time, when children are grown and worldly responsibilities are fulfilled, and there is nothing more for us to do here on earth other than fulfill our spiritual purpose. That is when we take up the mastery path and prepare to become a Servant of Love.

If you are reading these words, it is very likely that this applies to you. You cannot deny that you have heard the call to serve. You simply must decide if you are ready to answer it.

SALT AND LIGHT

Jesus told us that we are the salt of the earth. We are the ones who live simple, honest lives. We are not pretentious or full of pride. We do our best to keep the *Ten Commandments*, to worship God and to treat our brothers and sisters kindly.

We are the ones who model the teaching. Yet our voices are not heard in the land. Men and women less wholesome and peaceful than us make a greater stir, raising their voices and mounting the soapbox.

The world seems to reward them for their efforts. Name, fame and riches flow to them. Rewarded thus, they become even more corrupt—lying, cheating, stealing, and betraying each other.

These are the voices dominating the airwaves and teaching our children. How can we accept this? While it may not be easy for us to stand up and speak our truth, is it not our responsibility to bring our light into the affairs of everyday life? Is it not necessary that we become a mouthpiece for love and truth in our communities? Is it not time that we answer the call to become a Servant of Love?

Jesus told us we are the salt of the earth, but he also asked us, *"If the salt loses its saltiness, how can it be made salty again? It is no longer good for anything, except to be thrown out and trampled by men."* (Matthew 5:13)

People of faith must witness to that faith or the faith will die out. They must stand up and allow their voices to be heard so that the teaching of truth is not forgotten. Each generation has that responsibility. That is why Jesus told us clearly that we should not hide our light, but raise it up so that it can be seen. *"Let your light shine before men,"* he told us, *"that they may see your good deeds and praise your Father in heaven."* (Matthew 5:16)

One of the great challenges we face in walking the spiritual path is to be willing to stand up for the truth courageously, yet never to do so uncharitably. We do not stand for the truth when we need to make others wrong or cram the truth down their throats.

How we speak to others is as important as what we say to them. Recognizing that, we learn to stand up courageously, yet humbly. We respect the opinions of others and their right to decide for themselves. But we do not let their passion for their cause drown out our own voices, for those voices need to be heard.

There is a delicate balance to be found between being humble and being outspoken. Like a tightrope walker, each of us must learn to find that balance in our own way.

THE TEACHING OF TORAH

The teaching of *Torah* continues in each generation, for truth is constantly clarified and refined. Each generation is challenged to learn from the mistakes of the one before it and find new ways to understand, integrate and apply the insights of the ancient wisdom.

Much of what Jesus taught was pure Judaism. Jesus took long-winded statements and condensed them into their pure essence. His teaching claimed the heart center of Judaism and urged us to let the outer trappings go. Jesus was not interested in dogma. He was looking for truth.

We must do the same thing with the teaching that has come down to us through the Christian churches. We must learn to discriminate between the pure truth and the outer trappings. We must harvest the essence, the kernel, and throw the husk away.

However, the only way that we can properly discriminate between truth and falsehood is to put the teachings to work in our lives and see what brings us greater wisdom and happiness and what does not. We can argue about what is true until we are blue in the face and we will not come to agreement. That is because truth is both objective and subjective. It has a general relevance to everyone and a specific relevance to each individual. Both the objective and the subjective aspects of truth are important and need to be respected.

Universal truth is objective and it applies to all of us, regardless of which spiritual tradition we embrace. All of the great traditions share certain basic understandings about the nature

of God and the way that human beings can become more loving. That is why the great teachers of one tradition can embrace
the great teachings of another. Those truths are universal.

Differences between religions are subjective. Truth speaks to
one group of people in a slightly different language and with a
slightly different emphasis than it does to another. These differences can and should be respected.

In the same way, individuals within any given tradition hear
the truth of that tradition in different ways. Those differences
can and should also be respected.

Religious freedom means not only that each person is free
to choose his religion, but also that each person is also free to
understand the truths of that religion in a way that is unique
and meaningful to him. Churches and temples that offer that
kind of understanding and openness will attract more members
than those that don't.

The spiritual needs of most human beings are met when
room is made both for objective truth—the truth that speaks
to all of us—and subjective truth—the truth that speaks to our
individual consciousness at a particular time in our lives.

That is why it is helpful to live in a time when many teachings
are accessible to us. We can experiment and see what works for
us. We can more easily discern the timeless, universal truths that
weave through all the major religious traditions.

We can find a tradition and a community of worship that
works for us or we can create our own. But once we are done
exploring our options, the time for commitment comes. For
lest our intellectual quest for the truth leads us into spiritual

practice and the work of emotional healing, our lives will not be transformed by that quest.

We live in a time when there are many options. Sometimes that, in and of itself, can make it difficult for people to decide and commit.

Many people today are in recovery from old-guard, restrictive religious organizations. They are isolated as individuals and/or families and their needs for spiritual community are not met.

That is why it is so important for those who have leadership potential to stand up, share their hopes and their dreams, and begin to build spiritual community. Then, in the safe space of a community where people feel loved and accepted unconditionally, the real work of transforming hearts and minds can begin.

Today, we live in a time when the nuclear family structure is dissolving. Children and adults do not have the emotional and spiritual support that they need to live productive and meaningful lives. We are reaching a spiritual crisis of enormous proportions.

That is why the time has come for us to go beyond reading spiritual books and begin the work of building community from the ground up.

As Jesus told us, the time for hiding our light is over. It is time to stand up and allow our voices to be heard.

A UNIVERSAL TEACHING

The radical teachings of Jesus are universal teachings. They were given by Jesus to the Jewish people, but they were also given to others who had ears to hear them. The teaching could not by its nature be restricted by blood and birth and given only to a few. It had to be given to all people in all times.

If you are Jewish, you will have a natural affinity with this teaching for it is pure *Torah* and it unfolds directly from Jewish law. If you are a Christian, you will also have a natural affinity for this teaching for it is the essence of the gospels as they have come down to us. Others from different faiths may also resonate with this teaching and feel a love for Jesus as a teacher. That is because the truth that he teaches is universal—it is found in many traditions—and Jesus is an eloquent, compelling teacher of that truth. When people hear his words and feel his presence, they are called to God in a deep and profound way.

THE OPEN DOOR

Jesus was a master Rabbi. He was a lighthouse illuminating the darkness all around him.

Thanks to him, storm ravaged ships found safe harbor and the rejected and abused found sanctuary.

The arms of the master open wide to all who would take refuge in his heart and in the heart of his teaching.

And all of us—Christian, Muslim, Jew, Buddhist or Hindu, people of all faiths who believe in God and those who don't— all are welcome here.

The door to this house is always open.

"Ask and it will be given to you;
seek and you will find;
knock and the door will be opened to you."
(MATTHEW 7:7)

It is hard to find a teaching that is totally open to all men and women, regardless of who they are or what they have done, a teaching that invites everyone without exception into the circle of love.

Yet this is such a teaching. That is why it is so powerful.

And that is also why it demands so much of us.

To serve this teaching, you must leave behind every bias and prejudice that you have. You must surrender your envy, your pride, your jealousy, your anger, your shame, and your hatred. You must leave everything that is not love outside the door and enter the sanctuary with an open heart and an open mind.

Only when you come to God in this way can you meet the Son.

When you finally meet him you will see that he is not that different from you. He has all the sweetness of the human form, yet untrammeled by doubt, undistorted by fear. He shines with that hidden purity, that subtle light, that lives in the heart of each one of us.

In him, however, it has taken root and grown into a beacon, a bonfire, a light that burns steadily without consuming the Source that feeds it. For its fuel is love, formless, unconditional, limitless love.

As he looks at you, his eyes take you completely in. For he recognizes you as an equal brother, and yet he also sees your divine nature. On both accounts the recognition is true and clear and illumination comes as you begin to see yourself as he sees you.

Each of us is invited to this holy relationship in which we will learn to give birth to our True Self as He gave birth to His.

We call him Christ and it is to Christ that he calls us.

When the Son calls his brother, and his brother answers the call, his brother is redeemed, for he cannot answer the call and remain separate.

As the swimmer who jumps into the river is eventually carried to the sea, he who joins the Son also joins the Father, for the Father and the Son are one and the same.

That is how God becomes fully present, whether it is through Jesus, through you, or through me. When the persona steps aside, the divine Self is fully embodied.

That is the promise of this journey that begins in the dark womb of the Mother. And this is its shining fulfillment.

Namaste.
I bow to the Divinity within you.

NOTE TO THE READER

THIS BOOK rightly belongs to two important series of books that I have written: *The Spiritual Mastery Series* and *The Christ Mind Series*. Readers who find resonance with the teachings in this book will also enjoy the other books in both of these series.

The Books in the Spiritual Mastery Series include:

The Laws of Love
The Power of Love
The Presence of Love
The Gospel of Love (this book).

The Books in the Christ Mind Series include:

Love without Conditions
The Silence of the Heart
Miracle of Love
Return to the Garden
The Living Christ
Love is my Gospel (this book)

The Christ Mind Series also includes the following Compilations:

Reflections of the Christ Mind
I am the Door
The Way of Peace

Paul Ferrini is the author of over 30 books on love, healing and forgiveness. His unique blend of radical Christianity and other wisdom traditions goes beyond self-help and recovery into the heart of healing. His conferences, retreats, and *Affinity Group Process* have helped thousands of people deepen their practice of forgiveness and open their hearts to the divine presence in themselves and others.

For more information on Paul's work, visit the web-site at *www.paulferrini.com,* email: staff@heartwayspress.com or write to **Heartways Press, 9 Phillips Steet, Greenfield, MA 01301.**

Recent Releases from Heartways Press
Paul Ferrini's *Course in Spiritual Mastery*

Part One: The Laws of Love
A Guide to Living in Harmony
with Universal Spiritual Truth
144 pages $12.95
ISBN # 1-879159-60-0

Part Two: The Power of Love
10 Spiritual Practices that Can Transform
Your Life
168 pages $12.95
ISBN # 1-879159-61-9

Part Three: The Presence of Love
God's Answer to Humanity's Call for Help
160 pages $12.95
ISBN # 1-879159-62-7

Paul's In-depth Presentation of the Laws of Love on 9 CDs

THE LAWS OF LOVE
Part One (5 CDs) ISBN # 1-879159-58-9 $49.00
Part Two (4 CDs) ISBN # 1-879159-59-7 $39.00

Audio Workshops on CD

Seeds of Transformation:
5 cd set includes: Healing Without Fixing, The Wound and the Gift, Opening to the Divine Love Energy, The Laws of Love, The Path to Mastery.
5 CDs   ISBN 1-879159-63-5 $48.00

Two Talks on Spiritual Mastery
by Paul Ferrini
We are the Bringers of Love   CD 1
Surrendering to What Is   CD 2
2 CDs   ISBN 1-879159-65-1 $24.00

Love is That Certainty
ISBN 1-879159-52-X $16.95

Atonement: The Awakening of Planet Earth and its Inhabitants
ISBN 1-879159-53-8 $16.95

From Darkness to Light:
The Soul's Journey of Redemption
ISBN 1-879159-54-6 $16.95

Relationship Books

Dancing with the Beloved: Opening our Hearts to the Lessons of Love
ISBN 1-879159-47-3
160 pages paperback $12.95

Living in the Heart:
The Affinity Process and the Path of
Unconditional Love and Acceptance
128 pages paperback ISBN 1-879159-36-8
$10.95

Creating a Spiritual Relationship:
A Guide to Growth and Happiness for
Couples on the Path
128 pages paperback
ISBN 1-879159-39-2 $10.95

The Twelve Steps of Forgiveness:
A Practical Manual for Moving
from Fear to Love
120 pages paperback ISBN 1-879159-10-4
$10.95

The Ecstatic Moment:
A Practical Manual for Opening Your Heart
and Staying in It.
128 pages paperback ISBN 1-879159-18-X
$10.95

Christ Mind Books

Part 1   Part 2   Part 3   Part 4

Love Without Conditions ISBN 1-879159-15-5 $12.00
The Silence of the Heart ISBN 1-879159-16-3 $14.95
Miracle of Love ISBN 1-879159-23-6 $12.95
Return to the Garden   ISBN 1-879159-35-x $12.95

The Living Christ ISBN 1-879159-49-X paperback $14.95
I am the Door hardcover ISBN 1-879159-41-4 $21.95
The Way of Peace hardcover ISBN 1-879159-42-2 $19.95
Reflections of the Christ Mind hardcover $19.95

Wisdom Books and Audio

Everyday Wisdom
A Spiritual Book of Days
224 pages paperback $13.95
ISBN 1-879159-51-1

Wisdom Cards: Spiritual Guidance
for Every Day of our Lives
ISBN 1-879159-50-3 $10.95
*Each full color card features a beautiful
painting evoking an archetypal theme*

Forbidden Fruit: Unraveling the Mysteries
of Sin, Guilt and Atonement
ISBN 1-879159-48-1
160 pages paperback $12.95

Enlightenment for Everyone
with an Introduction by Iyanla Vanzant
ISBN 1-879159-45-7
160 pages hardcover $16.00

The Great Way of All Beings:
Renderings of Lao Tzu
ISBN 1-879159-46-5
320 pages hardcover $23.00

Grace Unfolding: The Art
of Living A Surrendered Life
96 pages   paperback   ISBN 1-879159-37-6 $9.95

Illuminations on the Road to Nowhere
160 pages   paperback
ISBN 1-879159-44-9 $12.95

Audio Books

The Economy of Love Readings from *Silence of the Heart, The Ecstatic Moment, Grace Unfolding* and other books.
ISBN 1-879159-56-2 $16.95

Relationship as a Spiritual Path Readings from *Creating a Spiritual Relationship, Dancing with the Beloved, Miracle of Love* and other books. ISBN 1-879159-55-4 $16.95

The Hands of God Readings from *Illuminations, Enlightenment for Everyone, Forbidden Fruit, The Great Way of All Beings* and other books. ISBN 1-879159-57-0 $16.95

Love Without Conditions Read by the author, 3 CDs.
3.25 hours ISBN 1-879159-64-3 $36.00
Also available on cassette tape for $19.95

Order any of these products on our website:
www.paulferrini.com

or call toll free in the US: 1-888-HARTWAY

The website has many excerpts from
Paul Ferrini's books, as well as information
on his workshops and retreats.

Be sure to request Paul's free email newsletter,
his inspirational weekly wisdom message,
and a free catalog of his books
and audio products.

Heartways Press, Inc.
9 Phillips Street
Greenfield, MA 01301
413-774-9474   Fax: 413-774-9475
www.heartwayspress.com
email: info@heartwayspress.com..

Heartways Press Order Form

Name _____

Address _____

City _____ State _____ Zip _____

Phone/Fax _____ Email* _____

Please include your email to receive Paul's newsletter and weekly wisdom message.

Title ordered	quantity	price

TOTAL _____

First Class Shipping: one book $5.95, two books $6.95   _____

3 books (shipped UPS ground) $7.95   _____

Additional books, (UPS ground) please add $1 per book   _____

TOTAL _____

For shipping outside the USA, or if you require rush shipping, please contact us for shipping costs.

Send Order To: Heartways Press, Inc. 9 Phillips Street,
Greenfield, MA 01301   413-774-9474
Toll free: 1-888-HARTWAY (Orders only)
www.Paul Ferrini.com   email: info@heartwayspress.com

Please allow 1–2 weeks for delivery. Payment must be made by check or credit card (MC/VISA/AmEx) before books are shipped. Please make out your check or money order (U.S. funds only) to Heartways Press, Inc.